Why Bitcoin is actually good for our planet. A sustainable and ethical revolution to the current financial system.

Reflecting about Cryptocurrencies and Bitcoin in 2021, ahead of a once in a lifetime opportunity.

Paperback Edition (English), 2021
Roberto Bourbon

Table of Contents

Introduction

Let's clarify one thing from the beginning. This book is not about *explaining* Bitcoin. Or Cryptocurrencies. We are not going to define or explain basic concepts linked to the Crypto world. In order to understand this book, you need to have some (very) basics about Crypto. I am assuming that whoever bought this book is already familiar with this world. If it is not the case, though, my recommendation is to do some quick research before reading it. You should know what cryptocurrencies are, what Bitcoin is and have some basic understanding of how the technology behind it, *the blockchain*, works.

Let me be clear. There is no need to be an expert of Bitcoin or Crypto to understand this book. Not by a long shot. However, if you have absolutely no idea what Crypto is, there is no real point in reading this book either, because a lot of concepts are given for granted.

We are going to explore the world of Crypto from a different perspective than what you usually find online, especially on Amazon Kindle. We are not going to talk about crazy price predictions or nonsense charts and trends. We are going to analyze Crypto (and in particular Bitcoin) purely from the perspective of an asset class. An asset class that, like all asset classes, has an ecological footprint. An asset class that is establishing itself in the financial world, at a pace rarely experienced before in the history of humanity.

There is a lot of buzz about Crypto, especially during the first months of 2021, with Bitcoin reaching 50,000 USD (and more!) per unit. As an author and investor, I always try to stay as much as possible neutral and cold minded in this context. I would lie if I told you that I am untouched by FOMO (fear of missing out) or by the scaremongering of *some* media. However, as always when I look to invest in something, I try to focus on the long term.

This is exactly what we will do in this book. We will try to look beyond the headlines and the claims that Bitcoin is an unsustainable, unethical asset. We will focus on what would be the implications of a world where Bitcoin is a mainstream asset, like gold. Then, we will imagine a world where Bitcoin not only is a leading *reserve* asset, but it is also a leading form of payment.

In doing this analysis we will also talk about the fundamental flaw of many (not all!) of the *naysayers* of Crypto. They tend to analyse an asset that is still in its very infancy, making comparisons with more mature, mainstream assets. We will see why this is not only unfair but outright idiotic.

By default, everything that we will see in this book is speculation. I will base myself on data as much as possible, but nobody can really know the future. This applies to Crypto as it applies to our current financial system. This book is also not intended to be financial advice. Mine is a reflection about the future of this fascinating asset and its implication on an ecological, societal level. It is not by any means an encouragement to buy (or not to buy) Bitcoin or any other financial asset.

Before closing this introduction, I want to spend a few words about the length of this book. This is not a long book. You can easily read it on a week-end or in a day. I am not a writer by trade, I am an investor. As such, I do prefer quality over quantity. I tend to go straight to the point and it is just not in my style to write a lot of pointless content. The result is a book of just above 14 thousands words, or around 30 pages in the paperback format proposed by Amazon.

I do know that psychologically when we buy a book we tend to be happier if it is longer than expected. I believe that I priced this book very fairly (just below 3 USD), exactly for that reason and to avoid people getting frustrated and leaving bad reviews. I do believe that most readers will actually be happy about reading this book and will realize the quality of the content rather than being disappointed with the "quantity" of it. However, if you do think you are not getting enough value for your money, please reach out directly to me and we can talk about it (more details in the last chapter of this book).

About the author

My name is Roberto and I am a self-published author on Amazon since 2020, passionate about politics and economics. I have extensive professional experience in multinational corporations and independent asset management.

I currently live in Switzerland and I have an exposure of around 5% to Crypto in my overall portfolio. The rest of my portfolio is well diversified with most of it exposed to US equity. By no means I am an early investor in Crypto, having entered this space only in the last couple of years.

I am also *not* a Crypto zealot. I do not believe that Crypto is the ultimate solution to all the problems of humanity. I try to get informed from as many sources as possible, do my own research and take a decision that directly affects my portfolio. Needless to say, the focus of this book is not about why I decided to invest in this space and whether you should do the same. It is rather a reflection of the future of Cryptocurrencies and Bitcoin in particular.

I do want to mention however that I am exposed to Crypto and I do believe strongly in its potential and future. I do not know how much Bitcoin will be worth in 1, 5 or 10 years. I do feel though that the world *might* be on the edge of an historical transformation. A transformation that will have rather *positive* implications for our planet.

Chapter 1
The fundamental flaw.

Let's start by analyzing why the argument of Bitcoin as an unsustainable resource is flawed from the very beginning. To better illustrate this flaw, we will use a short story.

Imagine being in 7,000 b.C. You are living in Mesopotamia, around modern day Iraq. Exactly like your parents and their parents, you are living as a hunter-gatherer. This means you find everything you need to survive in nature. As a nomad, you roam forests, lakes and plains with your family to hunt animals, eat mushrooms and fruits that you find in nature. It's the only way you have ever known to live, and it works fairly well. By constantly moving you ensure to always find a new source of food. The climate is also not an issue, since you can always move and stay in a temperate area as the seasons change.

Now imagine you hear about a different tribe, not too far from where you are at the moment, that lives in a very different way. Instead of constantly moving to find food and resources, they are always in the same place. They learned to *farm* food and live out of their harvest. Their tribe is also significantly larger than yours, actually being a composition of several tribes, all helping with the farming. As they need to withstand different seasons and have numerous people, their accommodations are larger, more solid than yours.

Imagine the tribe reaches out to you and your family and proposes for you to settle with them. Would you embrace this new way of living? Let me tell you, most probably not. The reason is that moving from a nomadic, hunter-gatherer life to a sedentary, agriculture-based society is extremely painful and risky.

For starters, your risk of starvation suddenly increases tenfold. If a harvest fails (which, no matter how good these people are at praying to the *right* gods, remains very likely) your family will not be able to live out of the food that the area can naturally provide. There are just too many people in the area for this to work, even assuming it will happen in the right season where there might be more fish in the river and mushrooms in the forest. In short, someone will surely die as soon as you experience crop failure.

This would be only the beginning of your troubles as a farmer. Illness is another big one. By living in confined, over-populated houses at close contact with animals, people here are getting sick much faster, with much worse sicknesses and literally die in flocks. Yes, the invention of agriculture is bringing in new illnesses. As hunter-gatherers, illnesses were either not mutating and transmitting from animal to human *at all* or, even if they did, remained confined geographically, given the low population density of any geographic region.

Another important element to consider before making the switch to agriculture is the sheer amount of work required. Crops need attention and hard work, constantly. Hunting-gathering might also seem hard work at a first glance, but it is not if compared to farming. You just need to constantly be on the move and nature fundamentally provides for you. Sure, you need to know how to hunt and which mushrooms won't kill you, but that's about it. Farming on the opposite is a new, unknown technique which requires constant work, 365 days per year.

It is even a different kind of work, physically. Hunting requires you to run fast for a short period of time and have good aim. On the other hand, harvesting a field requires you to have strength in your upper body and resistance over many hours of physical work. Speed and aim are worthless skills.

Then you come to consider your new potential diet. As a hunter-gatherer, you can enjoy a pretty diverse diet. Different animals, fruits, mushrooms and more, all depending on the season and geographical areas you are in a specific moment. Farming means eating almost exclusively one thing, which is whatever you are farming or harvesting. Your menu will consist of some kind of wheat and, if you are lucky, goat meat or milk twice per month. As a result, your physical shape will inevitably deteriorate.

There are actually studies showing that throughout the first thousands of years after the adoption of agriculture, the average height and weight of humans has significantly declined.

Ok, what does all this have to do with Bitcoin? Well, all the flaws that we have just seen for adopting agriculture are technically correct. Yes, shifting to agriculture would have meant for a nomadic person to have a poorer diet. Yet, this consideration misses the bigger picture.

Despite its flaws, agriculture eventually took over the world and kick started human society as we know it today. It allowed us, as a species, to produce a surplus of food for the first time in our history. This in turn allowed us to create cities, nations, empires. It allowed us to have specialized people fully dedicated to what we thought important. Researching new technology, praying to the gods to improve our farm yields, making war to our neighbours. Surely some (maybe most!) of the outcomes from our adoption of agriculture were horrible. As hunter-gatherers, an holocaust or a world war were simply unconceivable.

Overall though, we would have not evolved as a species and as a civilization without this crucial technology. Luckily we did adopt agriculture and the sacrifice of the millions of people that suffered under a structured, more "civilized" society were paid off in the long term with a radical improvement in our standards of living.

Now, do not worry though. I am not proposing that Bitcoin and agriculture are directly comparable. I personally think that while Bitcoin is surely remarkable, its impact on humanity will be *far - far -smaller* than that of agriculture.

Most importantly though, I do *not* think that adopting Bitcoin will trigger an immediate worsening of our living conditions as humanity and an improvement only visible in the long run. On the contrary, I believe that adopting Bitcoin will bring benefits that will be tangible and appear in our lifespans, with almost no drawbacks. We will see this in detail in the next chapter.

All I want to say in this chapter is that stating a true, negative fact - for example that Bitcoin requires a lot of energy to be mined - misses the greater picture. This is the fundamental flaw of the argument of Bitcoin as an unsustainable resource. Yes, Bitcoin might *seem* unsustainable (and it is not, as we will see shortly!) in the short run. Even assuming it is true, what is the alternative? Should we abandon any new technology or research because it consumes energy, regardless of its possible applications?

With this flawed logic we should then get rid almost completely of the airline industry because it is one of the most polluting industries in the world. Instead of researching new technologies that will allow us to achieve greener airplanes, we should destroy our standards of living until we live *truly* sustainably (which, not by a far stretch, would eventually mean returning to a small population of hunter-gatherers).

There are people that actually believe that the way to a more sustainable planet is to halt growth and development. I am definitely not one of them, but it is true that if we were to really live sustainably and assume no development in our technology, our standard of living would have to decrease massively. No travelling by plane *in your entire life*, for starters. No eating meat whatsoever. Solely relying on genetically modified soy and few other vegetables to eat (forget buying from local farms - that is not a sustainable option if everybody has to eat!). No showering, since water is a scarce resource in most of the inhabited world. No owning a car or possibly even an electric bike. No more children, because the ecological footprint of an additional human on earth is just massive. The list goes on.

It is not the point of this book to argue what a "sustainable" world would look like if current technology did not evolve. The point I am trying to make is that the only real solution to overcome ecological and societal challenges is technological advancement. I do not agree with anyone that disputes that. No amount of recycled plastic bottles can fix global warming. No amount of "sustainable" straws can stop the drop in ocean fish masses. The only solution would be massively diminishing our standard of living - which is a non-solution.

This has been true for the entire history of humanity. Going back to the agriculture example, we have seen how moving from nomadic society to a sedentary life has brought, for example, to the rise of new illnesses. This was a truly terrible consequence and humanity has had to deal with it until the invention of modern medicine (a new technology!), which in the great scale of things is literally yesterday. This withstanding, most people would agree that it was eventually a good choice for us to become a sedentary species, based on agriculture.

This same logic applies to all the arguments against Bitcoin that state a specific, negative fact about this Cryptocurrency. Sure, Bitcoin has been used and it is used for illegal purchases on the dark web. So what? Should we stop exploring this technology solely because of that? No. Not last because the bigger picture brings endless advantages for humanity. As we will see in the next chapter.

Chapter 2
<u>Bitcoin: more sustainable than the status quo</u>

We have just seen how most arguments that point at a negative fact about Bitcoin are fundamentally flawed, because they miss the bigger picture. Let's now focus on the argument that this book is really about: Bitcoin is unsustainable because it consumes a lot of energy.

In absolute terms, this argument seems to make sense. At the time of writing, in March 2021, it is estimated that Bitcoin consumes roughly the same energy as the entire country of Argentina on a yearly basis. This seems a really considerable amount of energy. The simple reality, though, is that all depends on what we are comparing Bitcoin against.

The gold mining industry, as a reference, has an estimated energy consumption that is roughly double the one of Bitcoin. Now, proponents of the argument of Bitcoin as a waste of energy would argue that gold has many more applications than Bitcoin and a much larger market capitalization. This is true, but again it is only its status as of today.

In a world where Bitcoin takes over gold as a reserve of value, the entire gold mining industry could easily disappear from the face of earth, along with its ecological footprint. This is because the (small) fraction of gold that is used in industrial applications right now could easily be absorbed by the gold that humanity has already mined.

The fact that Bitcoin will eventually replace gold is at all effects what most of the community around Crypto believes. This is not the place to argue in depth whether Bitcoin could completely substitute gold, however it is worth to quickly look at the fundamentals to see whether this scenario is plausible.

For a starter, Bitcoin is better at the only thing that makes gold a successful store of value: rarity. There will only be 21 millions of Bitcoin in existence, never more than this amount. The last Bitcoin will be mined around mid of the next century.

On the other hand, gold can be mined virtually indefinitely (at least in humanity's scale of time). More importantly, mining gold is subject to technological disruption. We will eventually be able to access asteroids and other planets in the next decades, or latest by the next century. Gold, along with other precious metals, might at that point be mined at scales never seen before, producing an over-supply and collapse in its price.

This might sound like sci-fi, at least to people working in the financial industry, but it is far closer than what we think it is. It might very well be possible that people alive today will see gold or other resources coming from asteroids or other planets.

Even if we do not manage to access gold outside of planet earth, new technology in mining might give us access to more gold on Earth. This is for example what happened with oil and fracking, a technology that made the USA a next exporter of oil after decades where it had not been the case. This problem with Bitcoin is simply non-existent, because the supply is limited to 21 million Bitcoins forever.

The other factor that might determine Bitcoin eventually "replacing" gold is the trust that people have in it. Trust in Bitcoin, ultimately, is really based on its rarity (since people only "trust" something because of its virtues). Exactly as trust in gold is based on its rarity or the trust in the US dollar is based on the faith in the organization that issues it (the FED, representing the most economically prominent nation in the world).

If we look at the history of Bitcoin in the last 10 years, we can already see how the adoption of this Cryptocurrency has scaled massively. We can effectively see four "stages" in the life of Bitcoin so far, corresponding to four waves of mass adoption.

In its first years of existence, only a few geeks would even know about Bitcoin. Famously, Wikipedia even deleted the page about Bitcoin in 2021, thinking it was a scam. These were the very early adopters, the people that barely knew what they were using and only grasped as pure theory the potential of Bitcoin. These are the years when a pizza was bought for 10,000 Bitcoins (the first purchase using a cryptocurrency!). Adoption in this first phase was limited to geeks, first movers, people that played with Bitcoin.

The second phase started shortly after, in the first half of the 2010s. The wave of adoption this time concerned people that used Bitcoins to... buy illegal stuff. This was the very *real* first use case of Bitcoin. It was (and still is, to some extent) the perfect way to buy something anonymously on the deep web. The users of this second phase were people that we might call criminals, or at the very least that wanted to do something illegal.

Then came speculators. The first wave of speculators, that is, corresponding to the third "stage" of Bitcoin's life. Starting from 2017, since Bitcoin overtook the 1,000 USD mark, an influx of (generally young) speculators started betting on the cryptocurrency, producing the 2017 Bitcoin bull run that peaked at around 19,000 USD at the end of 2017. These were the first "investors" in Bitcoin. Even if ultimately they were just speculating and producing a financial bubble as a result (which exploded in early 2018), they were the first ones to see Bitcoin as a store of value. This wave is perhaps the most important, because before then Bitcoin was really seen as something weird. After, people started reasoning about its fundamentals.

And so came the fourth (and last, for the moment!) stage of life of Bitcoin. Starting in late 2020, Bitcoin surged rapidly at its historical peek and went right through that, peaking in the mid-50,000 USD at the moment of writing in the first quarter 2021. What provoked this new bull run? A new wave of users, which I like to call "early institutional investors".

These include Tesla and Michael Saylor's Microstrategy, both listed companies that invested more than a billion in Bitcoin each. Rumors exist that many other companies might join the Bitcoin-craze, such as Apple or Oracle. JP Morgan, Goldman Sachs and all major banks are now actively *considering* Bitcoin, releasing statements, analysis and recommendations to their institutional clients.

This is happening because these companies are starting to see Bitcoin as a good store of value to "park" their hundreds of billions of US dollars. This fourth wave, in my view, was drastically accelerated by the 2020 pandemic and, most importantly, by the monetary measures that the FED and other central banks in the world have put in place.

At the moment of writing, significant inflation in consumer goods has not yet been seen in any major developed countries. However, the spectre of inflation has never been so present, possibly since the times of World War 2. This was triggered by money printing of the likes that have never been seen since decades. For reference, more than 70% of all US dollars ever printed in the history of humanity have been printed since March 2020. The risk that the US economy will experience inflation, making US dollars a terrible way to store value, has never been more concrete.

In this context, companies are "forced" to look at alternatives to their cash investment. This is why they started investing in Bitcoin (along with private investors and all of the previous users of the cryptocurrency), triggering the recent price hike.

We are still at early stages and chances are that it is not going to be an easy ride. Crypto remains a highly volatile asset that can lose 20% or 30% of value in one single day. However, if we look at the overall picture and at its history, it looks kind of like the "base scenario" that Bitcoin might slowly replace gold (and other assets, too!), becoming the ultimate store of value.

Even if nothing else happens and Bitcoin "just" becomes a mainstream means of storing value, the overall ecological impact of Bitcoin on the world would be positive. It would replace the gold mining industry, and possibly drastically reduce the silver mining as well, along with others.

The counter argument could be that some applications of gold and silver would remain. This is true, but it is unrealistic to think that the mining industries of these metals could survive by just serving the jewelry industry, along with limited industrial applications.

•

Personally, I believe gold will remain a store of value of some sort for the foreseeable future. This is unless we get to witness technology disruption of the likes we mentioned before (e.g. drilling asteroids). Unless that happens, gold will keep having a role in the finance world. At the same time though, Bitcoin will take over as the most prominent and efficient way of storing value. It is simply better in rarity, which is just what it really needs. And it is easier to "transport", being a digital currency with no physical limitations.

Until now we only talked about how Bitcoin could actually be a greener alternative to gold. However, this is kind of a "base scenario" for the king of cryptocurrencies. Bitcoin might go much further than replacing gold. It might even replace other means of payments and large corporations, such as Visa and Mastercard. It might replace traditional currencies (fiat currency, as the crypto world loves to call them) altogether.

Needless to say, Bitcoin's ecological footprint pales in comparison to that of the overall financial industry. Estimating the ecological footprint of these industries is tough, and not only because they are many and there are not necessarily clear statistics about them. It is difficult to estimate because we do not know what exactly they will be replaced with and at what pace.

For example, it is unrealistic to think that in a 50 year time frame Bitcoin could replace the US dollar. The USA is a very successful country and it will keep being so for the foreseeable future. Even if we forget about the USA, it is realistic to believe that 50 years from now we will still have *some* sovereign nations with their own currencies, worth *something*. In this sense, Bitcoin as *the only* currency of the world is simply not something we can realistically achieve in such a time frame. Of course, ultimately, nobody (including myself!) can predict the future. However, at the current status of things it seems unrealistic that state-nations will not exist in just a few decades from now.

Let's look at what's more achievable. It is more or less believable that Bitcoin might take away part of the role that the US dollar currently enjoys at global level. For example, in some developing countries the US dollar is currently used as de facto currency since the local currency is not considered reliable. This is particularly true in case of countries suffering from inflation and hyperinflation. Here, Bitcoin could play a role, becoming the de facto currency and replacing the US dollar in its function.

It would only make sense as Bitcoin is decentralized and therefore even more stable than the US dollar (which, in turn, it is more stable than local currencies of some developing countries, but still subject to the political will of the USA). The only barrier for Bitcoin (or other crypto) to become a de facto currency in developing countries is its adoption as a currency and acceptance in general commerce. As Bitcoin matures and becomes less volatile, more and more merchants might be willing to accept it as payment. Contrary to gold, which has a physical nature that renders it very impractical (it needs to be transported physically and weighted before using it for a purchase), Bitcoin is a virtual currency, with all the relative advantages in using it as currency. And it has another advantage. It is not subject to inflation *at all*!

There are currently already projects in the Crypto space that are specifically aimed at the developing world. Cardano (ADA) is one of them. This relatively new crypto currency is targeting Ethiopia and other African nations, trying to get deals with their governments and establish itself as the blockchain network on which their financial system is to be based. It is a very smart approach from the developers of this project, as they are looking at *proof of concept* in a real financial system.

Whether Cardano, Bitcoin or other cryptocurrencies will succeed remains to be seen. What is sure is that Bitcoin is the de facto "king" of cryptocurrencies, by market capitalization and global adoption. This puts Bitcoin in a very strong position, since the technology behind it is almost negligible. As long as it is "good enough" (virtually unhackable, decentralized, transparent), it will do a better job as a currency than anything else. No matter whether better technologies are behind other crypto currencies, the real deal when it comes to a financial system is *trust*. Something that Bitcoin is gaining quickly, more than anything else in the crypto space.

Another role that Bitcoin might "steal" from the US dollar is that of storing value. The US dollar, like any other Fiat currency, is a horrible way to store value. Yet, it is widely used to do so.

The reason why currency is an extremely ineffective way of storing value (much worse than gold) is, simply put, because of inflation. The average inflation rate in the USA during the 20th century was 8% on a yearly basis. Now, you could argue that this average is "artificially" increased by the two World Wars and going through a very turbulent century.

So let's take only inflation from 1980 to today as a reference. A 40 year time period. If you left 100 USD in a US bank account in 1980, in 2020 you would still see 100 USD of nominal value in your account. Yet, to have the same purchasing power, you would need around 315 USD. This means that you would have lost more than two thirds of your purchasing power by doing nothing. Inflation would have literally eaten your lunch.

Note that this calculation is done taking into consideration a time period of economic stability and prosperity, where there have been no major world wars. In this time frame we even experienced a financial crisis that brought the world to deflation for a few months at the end of the 2000s. Also it is done in USD, a currency that has remained dominant during that same time framework due to the USA being the dominant power in the world. If you did the same calculation on the Russian Ruble or virtually any other currency (except the Swiss Franc and few others), the results would have been much worse. You would have ended up losing up to 99% of value.

So, Fiat currency is a horrible way of storing value. Nevertheless, it is used by millions of individuals and thousands of corporations around the world to store value. From an individual perspective, part of the reason why currencies are used to store value is due to financial illiteracy. Many people consider investing in stocks or any asset in general as dangerous, due to volatility. They find solace in the fact of having a nominal value that is stable in time. 100 USD today is 100 USD tomorrow, *nominally*. Inflation is a difficult beast, because it does not manifest clearly, especially in developed countries with stable economies, where it is less than 3 or 4% yearly. Only after 10, 20 or 30 years you might realize how bad Fiat currency has been for you.

From the perspective of corporations, *cash* is used to store value for fiscal reasons or simply for lack of better options. Fiscally, many corporations rely on an intricate system of international subsidiaries to "optimize" taxation around the world. They escape from those countries that would tax their profits heavily, registering profits in those where they have special treatment or simply they can enjoy a better tax rate.

This is very good for the corporations' stakeholders (and completely legal, too), however it does not allow corporations to repatriate their profits to invest them. Many Tech giants have literally tens if not hundreds of billions of dollars "stuck" in countries where they have declared their profits, such as Ireland, Luxemburg or Singapore. They do invest in those countries (for example by building fancy offices to justify how and why their profits are taken there!), but there is only so much you can do that makes financial sense. They end up still being stuck with Billions in cash.

To be fair, lots of the cash that companies have is invested in "cash equivalents". These include governmental bonds and other financial instruments that have a short term expiration and can be liquidated fast and for cheap (hence, the name "cash equivalents"). These tools, however, are providing abysmal returns (if at all!) and, especially in recent years, are practically worse than having cash. This is why we end up with literally tons of cash that is sitting on the sidelines, slowly being eroded by inflation.

In this context, Bitcoin could take over the role of the US dollar as a store of value. For starters, it is a decentralized currency that can be freely purchased without any tax implication. Bitcoin is never physically in any legislation, that is until the person or company takes profit from it (if they ever do, as they could just use Bitcoin to purchase stuff... more on that later).

Then, thanks to its rarity (as we have seen before), it is an effective store of value, possibly better than gold in its fundamentals, even if still in its infancy and very volatile. In the long term, even if Bitcoin appreciates just enough to keep up with inflation, it is still way better than hoarding cash!

Finally, it has virtually no political risk. If you buy gold, it has to be stored somewhere and you are not only subject to taxation but also to physical risk. If you store gold in a country, the government at any point could always decide to seize it or tax it as wealth. Think it is not very likely? It has happened everywhere in the world throughout the 20th

Century, including in the USA in the 1930s with executive order 6102. It is a risk that you simply do not have with Bitcoin.

This all assumes a base scenario where Bitcoin exists just as a store value, as an alternative to gold. In this scenario, companies might find it sensible to put 5% to 10% of their cash in Bitcoin, effectively as a hedge against inflation. This is what's already happened with Tesla, for example, and seems to be happening with a few early movers in the corporate world.

When looked at from a long term perspective, this only makes sense because the only thing that needs to happen for it to be a wise investment is that Bitcoin beats inflation. That's a pretty low bar (especially when the FED is printing trillions of dollars each quarter), and many companies are starting to realize it. Still, it is not easy in heavily scrutinized and large companies to take what is still a very bold decision, that is buying Bitcoin. However I am convinced that as more companies add to the list of early movers, the more will come.

Things change radically if we assume that Bitcoin becomes not only a store of value but also a real currency, that can be exchanged for goods and services. In this case, corporations might not only decide to get *some* Bitcoin *in lieu of* gold. They might decide to move a considerable amount, if not most, of their cash to Bitcoin. For this to happen Bitcoin must become a "real" currency, that can be used to pay suppliers and perhaps even employees.

Back to individual investors now. Again, Bitcoin is still in its relative infancy but as it matures and its volatility diminishes, more risk averse investors might decide to hold it for the very same reason as corporations: it downright beats cash. It can appear absurd, today in 2021, to suggest that someone as a retiree would decide to hold Bitcoin. Today, this would be a high risk and definitely not something I would even think about if I was a retiree.

However, in 10, 20 or 30 years from now, things might have changed drastically. If Bitcoin will have proven to be an effective alternative to gold *and/or* cash, it would only make sense for a retiree to have it. Maybe even hold mostly Bitcoin in their portfolio.

Especially if they will be able to use it to pay for their winter cruises or retirement home and not only to beat inflation.

As in the case of gold, the realistic future is that Bitcoin will be accompanied by the US dollar (and other Fiat currencies), rather than substituting them. At least for the foreseeable future. It will not replace everything all of a sudden, but rather slowly.

Let's think for a second about the ecological implications of this scenario. Millions of corporations, financial institutions and retail investors using Bitcoin. Yes, Bitcoin will have a quite significant ecological footprint. But it might have substituted many, more polluting industries.

No more ATMs. No more Credit Cards. No more thousands of different legacy software running in thousands of different banks that deal with and manage virtual currency of their retail clients. Everything on one blockchain. Drastically reduced frauds, as everything is decentralized and fully transparent, virtually unhackable. The benefits add up quickly. It is really hard to argue that a transition to Bitcoin, even if slow or partial, would not be good for our planet.

Before closing this chapter, I would like to make a couple of other considerations. First of all, the ecological footprint of Bitcoin is only "bad" if the energy that Bitcoin uses is produced with non-renewable resources (e.g. burning coal or oil).

Let's take electric cars as an example. They do not get a bad ecological reputation at all, but they are exactly in the same situation as Bitcoin. They will only be better for the planet if the energy that is used to power them is produced *sustainably*. And this does not even consider the ecological footprint of producing, maintaining and recycling batteries.

Governments are pushing the adoption of electric cars like crazy, especially since the current pandemic. As an example, the UK is planning to ban the sale of traditional fuel-powered cars by 2035. The European Union is following the same path, with strict regulations that might even ask for 0 emission to all new cars sold in Europe at the end of the current decade. Incentives to the automotive sector during the pandemic have been granted largely on the promise of selling more and more 0-emission vehicles.

For the record, I am a big fan of electric mobility and I do think that this is the future of the automotive industry. However, I do not understand how (almost) everyone is failing to discuss their biggest challenge: how do we power them with green energy?

The real political debate shouldn't be about banning the sale of fuel-powered cars (or whether we should ban Bitcoin because they consume energy). It should be about how we plan to make our energy production model sustainable at scale. This is a topic that goes well beyond the purpose of this book. It is sufficient to say that there are huge challenges when it comes to transforming how a large country generates its energy. Especially when the public has been indoctrinated about how nuclear is dangerous and how we can just magically build windmills and solar panels to do it. So, why aren't we talking about this, instead of pushing electric cars blindly and just "moving" the problem upstream?

Again, I am a big fan of electric mobility and I believe that pushing for mass adoption is the right thing to do. Exactly how Bitcoin is also good. The solution to how we generate energy sustainably will come with time and with technological advancement.

However, I see a clear hypocrisy in being all in favor of electric mobility but completely against Bitcoin, while they share the same fundamental issue. The reason why this happens (or at least my guess) is that pushing electric cars is ultimately good for the economy, good for employment and better for the politicians that want to be re-elected. The broader ecological picture does not interest them and it is therefore not pushed to the public as much.
On the other hand, Bitcoin is not understood yet by the high majority of the population and it has virtually zero impact on politicians' chances of getting re-elected. It is easy to understand then how any argument can be used against it, including the fact that it consumes too much energy.

Ultimately, the scale of energy consumption of Bitcoin is difficult to grasp, simply because its applications today are still up to debate. If Bitcoin really is just little more than a *meme* or a hobby for nerds, then it becomes difficult to justify its ecological footprint. The real question then becomes what can Bitcoin become and not how much it consumes today. In this context, energy consumption by itself is not enough of an argument to decide not to pursue a new technology, as we will see now in the next chapter.

Chapter 3

Stuck in the African plains

We have already seen in Chapter 1 how the fundamental flaw of most arguments against Bitcoin is that they do not consider the bigger picture and potential long term benefits of the cryptocurrency. In this chapter, I want to briefly explain why bringing up the ecological footprint of any resource, asset or project is utterly meaningless and counter productive.

Any big innovation in the history of humanity has had a big "setup" cost. Hell, even in the business world any innovation comes with a big upfront expenditure. This is called "Capital Expenditure" (or CAPEX for short). If a company wants to innovate a product or services, they usually need to invest money to do so, *before* they see any benefits.

Let's take the example of electric cars again. Let's say that I am a car manufacturer that really cares about electric mobility and I want my full car line up to be electric in 10 years. I will need to heavily invest in order to be able to do so. For starters, I will need to build a factory to produce batteries and find new suppliers for raw materials to produce those batteries. Then, I will need to completely restructure part of my existing factories. Assembling thermic engines is a very different matter than plugging batteries into car frames. I will also need to also do hundreds of other smaller investments, from software to control the electric motors to purchasing electric cables.

Overall, I will have a lot of work to do and a very heavy bill to make it happen. I might end up having to spend hundreds of millions if not a few billions dollars. That might even be more than the profit I currently generate in 1, 2 or 5 years. So, should I give up before I even start? The answer is, *it depends*. It depends on what the long term returns on the investments are. No business would ever take a decision to invest (or not invest) in something purely based on the absolute amount of money that needs to be invested.

As a car manufacturer, I might decide to invest billions in capital expenditure if I believe that electric mobility is indeed the future and that this will put me ahead of competitors in 5 or 10 years time. I might not even have a choice, for example if enough governments mandate that I will only be able to sell electric cars as of a certain date. On the other hand I might decide not to invest and keep producing fuel-powered vehicles forever, if I think that electric mobility will never really be mass adopted.

When we look at Bitcoins, the situation is the same. Should we ban Bitcoins because they consume energy? Well, this is a non-question. It cannot be answered, because it depends on what are the future benefits of Bitcoins. By only considering the ecological footprint of Bitcoin, we are effectively only seeing one side of the equation. We cannot solve this equation unless we manage to quantify the benefits of Bitcoin. We have already seen this concept in the previous chapter. What we have not mentioned is that it is almost impossible to quantify the benefits of Bitcoins today.

The benefits of most technologies are impossible to quantify until much, much later than when they are launched. Literally every big innovation in the history of humanity had a rough start, huge upfront investment and as humanity we only saw their benefits after years, decades or even centuries they were introduced. As humanity, we should *try* new technologies *until the technology is proven useless*, not avoid technologies until they are proven useful. Why? Because there is no other way to do things. Let's look at what history might teach us.

We have already seen the example of agriculture in chapter one. Agriculture was a horrible deal when it was invented. The reality is that for millennia most of humanity suffered because of it. If we exclude the small percentage of population that lived better because of it (noblemen, clergy, merchants), most people suffered plagues, fatigue and an incredibly short lifespan because they were forced to work in the fields to sustain themselves and the minority. This was not the case as hunter-gatherers, where everything was provided naturally to us, with relative ease.

We can take any other big innovation in the history of humanity and observe a similar situation. Let's take for example the Industrial revolution. Once again, the industrial revolution was a horrible deal when it was invented. People had to cram into overpopulated cities, living in horrible hygienic conditions, barely able to afford to eat with their salaries and working 90+ hours work weeks. Was it worth it? Not for the generations of people that were born and died into this system before we started seeing progress. Surely their sacrifice was worth it for us, enjoying the benefits of industrialization and having learned from our mistakes.

One could argue that, as human species, we only really saw the benefits of agriculture and the industrial revolution (or any other major technological breakthrough) in the last few decades. Until the early 20th Century, most humanity was still living in absolute poverty, for the benefit of a very limited number of elite people (not noblemen anymore, but mostly capitalists). We really only dramatically elevated our standards of living after World War 2. Still, until 30 years ago almost half of humanity lived in absolute poverty. And even today there are still hundreds of millions of people that suffer from hunger and live in absolute poverty, even if they are not even close to represent the majority of the world's population.

If the only thing we cared about was the standard of living of the average human on planet earth, then we were probably better off as hunter gatherers in the african plains. Only in very recent years *most* (not all!) of humanity has come to live in better conditions than our ancestors hunting gathering ancestors.

Of course things change if we throw other factors into the equation. Without agriculture and the industrial revolution we would not have witnessed the creation of art, literature, poetry, architecture, philosophy and science. We would have not gone to the moon, we would not have started exploring space, we would have not evolved as society overall. If we are to continue on the trajectory of exponential development we experienced in the last 100 years or so, it's possible that the real benefits of most of humanity's technological innovations have not even fully manifested yet.

If you took a snapshot of humanity in any moment of time since 5,000 b.C. to 1900 A.D., you would observe a similar picture. The vast majority of humanity was suffering, either because of war, famine, sickness or a combination of all those elements. A tiny fraction of humanity was, on the other hand, living a decent life. Literates, noblemen, clergy. Their lifestyle was rendered possible by the sacrifice of the many. Was it worth it? Again, if you asked a peasant from the 8th Century, who was raised the son of a peasant, maybe not. If you see where we came today as a society, maybe yes.

Before we go back talking about Bitcoin, I want to make another point. The true benefits of a technological innovation are always impossible to assess until much later than when this is invented, no matter the type of innovation. This applies to massive breakthroughs such as agriculture or the industrial revolution, but it does as well to more "mundane" innovations.

Let's take cars. When the first cars were invented, at the end of the 19th Century, they were extremely expensive, slow, inefficient. Not to mention they needed fuel to work, which was not easy to buy without a network of gas stations. Cars really only became useful tens of years after they were first commercialized. There were a lot of very knowledgeable people in the 1800s and early 1900s who hated cars and sincerely thought they could not possibly replace horses.

The first "boom" of the automotive sector was actually triggered by World War I. Engines, cars and the first tanks were developed with the specific objective of killing people. And if not to kill them directly, to at least support a war machine whose objective was explicitly to kill the enemy (such is the case of the first ambulances, for instance, deployed in war zones to evacuate wounded soldiers).

So, should humanity have stopped the production of cars in the 1920s because they had applications in war? Let's forget about the ecological footprint of the automotive industry (obviously at the time climate change was barely theorized, let alone a public concern). War was a huge concern for the public opinion post-WWI. And for a good reason. Millions of people had just perished and the public (at least in Europe) was suddenly realizing they did not like war after all. Diesel and petrol engines were quite literally the engines of War. Used in tanks, trucks and planes they were the backbone of modern armies. Without them, a war was impossible.

Yet we did not stop developing this technology. What happened? World War II. Tanks and planes had even more of a central role of what they had in World War I. Even more people perished. Technically, Nazi Germany would have not been able to invade Poland, attack Russia or capitulate Paris without tanks, planes and trucks.

So, should have we stopped developing this technology (assuming that would have even been possible, which it was not)? After more than 80 years we can safely say that no, we shouldn't have, even if in the short term a lot of bad things happened. Engines, cars and trucks had a huge positive role in the decades after World War II. Surely from an economical standpoint, since the civil automotive industry really became one of the backbones of modern nations. As well as from a standard of living standpoint, since most people in developed countries started buying cars and enjoying freedom of movement like never before.

The same rationale applies to planes. Or to computers! When Microsoft kickstarted the PC revolution in the 1990s, computers were large, expensive, inefficient (albeit already much better than their predecessors from the 1980s or 1970s!) and largely useless. Their applications were limited to a very few professions and use cases. Sure, if you happened to be working at an M&A department in a Wall Street firm you already *needed* a computer to run your simulations.

However, many professions that today you cannot do without a computer did not even exist as they do today (for example the graphic designer). For the general public computers were just useless. Yes, you could already use the internet, but for what? Looking at a bunch of websites (assuming you knew their URL, anyway). But you would have found no information that you could not find on a good old school encyclopedia. Playing some video games. But nothing you could not have played on a (less expensive) game console. Writing a virtual document. Nothing you could not have typed on a typewriter, which would have had the benefit of saving you the time to find a printer to actually get a real, usable, paper document in your hands.

Had climate change been a trending topic back then, an argument could have been made that computers were a total waste of energy and were unsustainable. They surely were considered by some at least a waste of money, time and resources. And that is because they were! It would have made total sense to give up on computers and just use the best technology previously available to do the (few) jobs of a modern computer. Typewriters, gaming consoles, encyclopedias. They all existed, they all were widely and successfully used and they would have eliminated the need of having a new technology that was a waste of resources.

Only after years, if not decades, computers really became central in our life. They evolved into personal devices and smartphones, exactly like the first goofy cars evolved into trucks, tanks, more efficient cars, taxis and UBER. They ended up revolutionizing our life. In the process we had plenty of horrible applications of computers. The internet eased illegal trafficking of all sorts. Smartphones were and *are* making us dumber (at least according to some researchers). This is just to mention two of the "negative" applications of computers, at the antipodes one from the other. However, they also found their applications in virtually any industry in the world, incrementing our productivity and giving us powers that we never had before. They granted us access to virtually all the knowledge of the world in the palm of our hands and helped keep us connected with the people we care about in the process.

Was it worth it to keep developing computers for decades, despite their few initial use cases and obvious limitations? Yes it was. Even in the 1970s the potential of computers was clear in the eyes of people that were working in the industry. Many people might have hated the technology and called it a waste of time and money throughout the years, but computers thrived nevertheless.

The same applies to digital cameras, which when they were first commercialized on a large scale in the 2000s were expensive and vastly inferior to traditional cameras. Only after years they ended up being integrated in smartphones and completely disrupted the industry. The same applies to many more minor inventions as well.

Ok, Back to Bitcoin now. What are the benefits of Bitcoin and (especially) the blockchain in the long term? I have no clue! Believe me, if I had a clear idea I would not be writing eBooks on Amazon.

Whoever claims to know the future applications of the blockchain is either lying or plain stupid. We cannot possibly understand how Bitcoin and the blockchain will shape our world today, in 2021. Exactly how we could not understand how computers would have changed our lives in 1990. We can imagine the ways this technology will be applied, but ultimately we simply do not know. In the 1990s very few people envisioned a world where computers were in the palm of our hands. Even those who did could not really grasp what we would have done with them.

We mentioned a few possible applications of Bitcoin in the previous chapter. Replacing gold seems kind of a "base scenario" based on what we know today. Even if Bitcoin will end up not having any other role in the world, its ecological footprint would be justified. The reality though is that its applications are probably many more.

This is all to say that we cannot stop the development of Crypto just because it has a large ecological footprint based on its applications *today*. Yes of course Bitcoin seems kind of pointless today, as all technologies had before it seemed. But this is only one side of the equation. We need the other side of the equation to really be able to assess the situation. Sadly, we won't get the other side of the equation until years, decades or possibly centuries from now.

If we had stopped the development of any technology because we did not grasp all of its applications immediately, we would have never perfected airplanes to fly. We would have never had an industrial revolution. We would have never invented agriculture. We would have never even moved from the african plains where the first *homo sapiens* developed. We would still be stuck as hunter gatherers in the same region where our ancestors were born. After all, why even venture outside a few safely inhabited valleys? It surely comes with a great effort and risk. Not to mention its ecological footprint.

Chapter 4
But Bill said so!

I was very surprised to see how Bill Gates joined the crypto skeptics in recent months. Especially because one of his arguments indeed concerned how Bitcoin is unsustainable from an ecological standpoint.

To be clear, I do admire Bill Gates and all of its life work. We mentioned in the last chapter how only a few people in the 1990s had a clear idea of the possible implications of computing. Bill Gates was one of them. Watching his interviews from the mid-1990s is something I can only recommend. Among other things, he basically theorizes the existence of smartphones 20 years before their existence. It is truly an humbling experience to see how lucid and what a visionnaire he was. This makes even more surprising how someone of his caliber would be skeptical about Bitcoins and neglect to mention the blockchain as a game changing technology.

I am also equally impressed by his work in the last decade or so. Moving his focus and life work from tech to eradicating the world's worst disease is nothing that does not deserve my utmost respect. I am dedicating a chapter to discuss his opinions precisely because of the respect I have for him.

It is normal to see bankers and people in the financial world being skeptical about Bitcoin and cryptocurrencies. However, these people generally have created close to zero value for the world in their whole lives. They operate in an industry based on old, antiquated values and views.

Most importantly, history is littered with obvious examples of how the mainstream financial industry is chronically incapable of recognizing and understanding real value in the world. A few examples? Amazon was ridiculed by all major banks and agencies for years and years, until it became the behemoth that is today. All of a sudden agencies and analysts started issuing "buy" recommendations for Amazon, once it already rallied 1000% or more. The same is happening at the moment with Bitcoin and Cryptocurrency, with a few prominent banks starting to release analysis and recommendations about the space (10 years after it was created and ridiculed or ignored).

Another obvious example is how the financial industry was so narrowly focused on the short term that it literally risked to collapse on itself during the 2008-2009 crisis. Let's forget about rating agencies being unable to do their jobs. We are talking about Lehman Brothers declaring bankruptcy and Goldman Sachs being rescued by Warren Buffet to not see the same faith. We are talking about companies that are so badly managed and in such a consistent way that they literally risk failure because of their own mistakes.

The financial industry is simply structured in a way that is incapable to recognize value or really understand anything of the real world. They quite literally would not be able to make money in a different way than what they are used to even if they started to crap gold.

It is not a surprise then that many Crypto skeptics come from this industry. Their arguments vary and sometimes can also be interesting. Overall though, I do not want to give weight to an industry that has again and again proven to be incapable of generating value for itself, let alone for the world.

On the other hand, an argument against Bitcoin coming from Bill Gates, a tech visionnaire, is a different thing. A thing that I, personally, do not agree with, but that I do believe is worth to spend some time to discuss.

_____

To start the discussion, let's try to understand what exactly Bill Gates said about Bitcoins. As much as I can understand from the news, he used two different arguments against Bitcoin.

The first is that Bitcoin is ineffective as a financial instrument. In his own words, that is because "Bitcoin uses more electricity per transaction than any other method known to mankind, and so it's not a great climate thing".

The second argument is that it is a fundamentally risky asset and people should be wary of it. Again, in his own words, referring to Tesla's recent purchase of Bitcoin: "Elon has tonnes of money and he's very sophisticated, so I don't worry that his Bitcoin will sort of randomly go up or down [...] My general thought would be that if you have less money than Elon, you should probably watch out".

Let me start by saying that I partially agree with this second argument. Bitcoin is extremely volatile and has a very short history when compared to more traditional assets such as stocks or bonds. If we compare it with gold then, its history pales as gold has been used by humanity as a store of value for thousands of years.

It is true that nobody (if not a very few educated investors) should even think about having a position in cryptocurrency in their portfolio of above 5% or 10%. The reality though is that many people, especially young investors, are piling on cryptocurrency. Some people have crypto as the only asset they own. This is dangerous, given the high volatility of this asset class. It is especially stupid for people that have almost no savings, no financial safe net and a low paying job. We are after all talking about investing into an asset that could easily depreciate by 50% or more in a week or a month.

Even if this book is obviously not to be considered financial advice by any means, I personally would never recommend any young person to invest more than 5% or 10% (at cost basis!) of their portfolio into crypto. Exceptions might exist - yes, if you have 10 million net worth at 35 years of age, you might YOLO 5 millions into crypto - but we are talking about educated investors, not your average Joe.

To be fair, even older investors are exposed to the risk of Bitcoin. In this regard, it would be very unwise for a retiree or someone that needs to live out of its investment portfolio to be too much exposed to crypto.

The fact is that Bitcoin is still a young, volatile and therefore risky asset. At the same time it is undoubtedly becoming "mainstream". This indeed exposes a lot of people to risk, as they might get into the crypto space purely out of FOMO (Fear of Missing Out), without understanding it and just for highly speculative purposes.

It can be an issue to have many unsophisticated investors entering a new space without carefully considering its risk. In this sense I do agree with Bill Gates. There is too much hype about Bitcoin and people are getting into it without the proper research or caution. However, that fact does not make Bitcoin *per se* something that we should forget about or that is inherently risky.

What I do not agree with, is Bill Gates's first argument. In my humble opinion he is making at least one huge mistake. He states that Bitcoin is inherently inefficient to do financial transactions because it uses a lot of energy to do so. In doing so, however, he does not consider Bitcoin's future applications and how a Blockchain-based world will look like.

Let me illustrate what I mean with an example. Let's say that it is 1994 and you are selling your car to your neighbour. You have a computer and you are considering using it to write the contract you will use to sell the car.

Is this an efficient decision? Remember, it's 1994. I can tell you that this was not an efficient way to write a contract *at all,* in 1994!

First of all, because after having written the contract you would have to print it to give it to your neighbour and close the deal. Assuming you would even have a printer at home, this is a total waste of energy *and* time since you could have just used paper and pen in the first place! Secondly, because by using a pen or a typewriter you would not consume *any* energy if not the one coming from your fingers. Again, a waste of energy.

Time-wise this decision sucks as well. In the case of the typewriter you are not even required to spend more time writing the contract than what you would have spent using the computer. As a matter of fact you would probably spend less time with the typewriter because with the computer you are wasting time turning it on and opening the right editing software.

Now, let's forward to 2021. You are in the same situation. Would you use a computer to write a contract to sell your car? Of course yes. This makes sense now because you are putting productivity into the equation.

First of all, you could look for a contract template on the internet, saving you time when compared to writing the contract from scratch. Second, you could send the contract to the buyer without printing it (saving time, energy and money). After all, as long as you both have a digital copy on your respective computers, that's good enough. An additional benefit is that you could have someone review the contract without needing to re-print it and correct it manually. Finally, you could also store it on the cloud for much more time and at a lower cost than before, with a significantly lower risk that it gets lost next time you are moving houses.

The reality is that today you really have no choice than using a computer for this use case. Even if you did not want to use it, who even has a typewriter anymore at home? And who is going to take a hand-written contract seriously anymore? Computers have become the norm, slowly but surely. There is an entire new ecosystem around computing that simply did not exist 27 years ago. This makes using a computer the most efficient choice for a lot of things.

Does this mean that 27 years you would have actually been better off using a computer than a typewriter? No, it doesn't. You would have been a geek for using a computer for such an application. You would have done it more because you felt "cool" than for any real advantage. Most people in the world wouldn't even have had the choice to use a computer to write a contract in 1994, simply because they did not have access to one.

Let's take another example. Let's say you are an entrepreneur, owning a small business. Is it efficient to use a computer to do the simple accounting for your small enterprise? It does, only because you enjoy many benefits from it in terms of productivity. For a starter, you can store your historical accounting data. You can also use a software to help you with the calculation and reduce the possibility of committing mistakes. Then, you can send the data to the government when you have to pay taxes.

All these applications were invented much later than the computer that allows you to do simple accounting. Again, in the early 1990s you would have probably been better off just using paper and a calculator to do the accounting at a small firm, if anything for the mere cost of a computer. Today is ridiculous to even think about not using a computer.

This is all to say that if you look at the single applications without considering the bigger picture, computers are a horrible way to do things (as is Bitcoin). Even today, we use computers for extremely inefficient use cases. Take reading a book. Is it really energetically and environmentally OK to use a tablet to read a book? It depends. Assuming that all the books you read are printed on recycled paper, you can probably buy thousands of them before you recover the ecological footprint of buying a single tablet. However, using a tablet to read books makes a lot of sense when you consider the bigger picture. A tablet allows you to do other things than just reading a book. A tablet allows you to have hundreds or thousands of books in the same place, making it perfect for a long holiday where you might want to read a lot.

This is why I do not agree with what Bill says, even if I highly respect him as someone that has contributed more than most people to the advancement of the human species. He is not considering the big picture, when looking at Bitcoin.

Chapter 5
Under our noses

If the examples of the previous chapter are not good enough, we can think about this from another angle. Fundamentally, a technology is only as good as the ecosystem in which it is used. Let's take our most sophisticated and advanced rocket today. It is a marvel of engineering and we use it to supply the International Space Station and launch satellites.

Let's now imagine sending this rocket back to Paris in 1200 A.D, during the Middle Ages. Let's assume that along with the rocket we also sent more than enough fuel, a team of engineers, a launch pad and a bunch of computers. Basically everything you need to operate it. That rocket would be by far the most advanced form of technology on the planet at that time. However, would that be of any use? No, it wouldn't. There would not be an International Space Station. There would be no point for that rocket to be launched just to become a space detritus. If the unlucky engineers we sent back with the rocket want to survive, they should probably start thinking about how to re-invent themselves as war engineers and scrape everything they have to make war machines. That rocket would be a marvellous technology, albeit completely useless in that context and technological ecosystem.

The same applies to any other technology. Would the fastest of our MAGLEV trains be of any use at the time of the Roman Empire under Julius Caesar? No, it wouldn't. It would be unable to literally serve any purpose without a network of high speed railways. The Romans would never think to waste time, energy and money to build another one.

That's why we cannot measure a technology based solely on its applications *and* efficiency at the time it is first invented or applied. As time passes, technologies mature becoming more efficient and finding more applications. With enough time, they end up building an ecosystem of technologies that changes our world, disrupting and substituting old technologies altogether in the process.

It happened to humanity at a speed never seen before during the last 200 years or so. It happened with an almost exponential speed as well.

From the invention of agriculture to the industrial revolution several thousands years passed (5 to 10 thousands years, depending on which historian you ask). During this time frame humanity was substantially unchanged, from a technological and societal perspective. Sure, many minor technologies were invented and our cultures changed completely, many times. Culturally, the population of Babylonia in 2400 b.C. had nothing in common with 17th Century France. Exactly like the ancient Romans had nothing to do with the Azteks or the Chinese under the Ming dynasty.

However, from a purely societal perspective nothing *really* changed and these societies were all the same. At the bottom we still had the vast majority of the population working in the fields to maintain an elite of few. Throughout the millennia we invented better ways to kill each other. We had the time to fill thousands of librarieries with new literature. We had time to invent new religions, new social norms and ultimately new excuses to justify the exploitation of the masses. Ultimately though we were still all collectively "slaves" of our latest great technology, agriculture. This was the common denominator of all populations in the history of humanity, until the industrial revolution.

After the industrial revolution, It took a good 100+ years for our world to change from agriculture based to factory and output based. It took a relatively short time for a minority of people to be able to maintain a majority thanks to technology. We were freed from our agricultural chains, after millennia. The sacrifice of our ancestors ultimately paid off. In the process of freeing ourselves from our chains we invented new ideologies, too. This was needed to cope with this new revolutionary technology and the subsequent radical change in our society. In a world where output was key and abundance was a possibility, stories about the natural order of things just did not appeal to us anymore. So we invented capitalism, communism and various sub-ideas such as the various nationalisms. We throwed away thousands of years of stories and societal norms in a short period of time, simply because it was the obvious thing to do.

After the industrial revolution, the pace of innovation really accelerated. It took less than 50 years for planes, cars and trains to see mass adoption and drastically change the way we travel. The pace of change was so fast that these two technologies are barely 100 years old and we are already considering throwing them under a bus. Why using planes if you could use hyperloops, cutting on travel times and improving the ecological footprint of travelling? Why using cars when it would be much more efficient to summon self driving electric vehicles when we need to move from A to B? Cars and planes already changed drastically in their relatively short lifespan and they now seem to be on the verge of changing again or be abandoned altogether.

If we look at the last few decades, the pace of change has only accelerated further. It took no more than 20 years for computers and the internet to become mainstream and completely change how we interact with each other. From nothing more than a curiosity to the very basis of our society today.

Technological advancement and subsequent societal change happened many times in the past. Yet, many of us still fail to understand this process and prefer to be skepticals about new technologies until proven wrong (which they usually are, faster than ever before).

What I personally find unbelievable is that most people in the financial and business world would totally agree with the fact that our world is changing at a faster and faster pace. This is, as a matter of fact, one of the most common and "cheap" concepts you will hear in the business world today. Visit the website of any large corporation or financial institution and you will find plenty of references to how they are adapting to an ever changing environment. Read the yearly shareholders' letter of any listed company and you will be promised how the firm is embracing change, adopting new technologies and readying itself to compete in this new century.

Yet, the vast majority of these companies are unable to see and recognize change when they have it literally under their nose. I already spent a few words on how hilarious the world of finance is and how clearly inept are the people working in it, even by their own standards. That is why we still see people and companies talking about change being skeptical about Bitcoin, Crypto and the blockchain.

When we look at Bitcoin today, we do have a clear application of this asset (and technology) that is taking over: to be a store of value and, by a stretch, a substitute of (or at least part of) our financial system. It is therefore clear to me that Bitcoin has already great potential and much more is coming in the next few years.

How long will it take to blockchain to really revolutionize our world? Obviously I cannot say (and nobody else can, at this stage). What we can do, however, is again looking at the past for inspiration. It is really impressive how far Bitcoin has already come in its first 10 years of life.

Let's look at the facts. What started as little more than an experiment is now being purchased *in billions* by publicly listed companies. This by itself is an impressive achievement. Despite what banks might or might not say (they will anyway change their minds as soon as they can make money out of their newly formed opinions), Bitcoin is already an alternative to gold or fiat currency - albeit a risky and highly volatile one.

Let's compare Bitcoin (or, better, the blockchain) to the last wave of disruptive technological innovation we experienced, which is to say computers and the internet. The very first computers were created in the 1950s, but it wasn't until the 1970s that they started to find the first applications in research and the military. From there, it still took them around 20 years to be introduced to the public (which is, in the early 1990s). That was the time when the internet also started to be used by the public. It then took 10-20 years for these two technologies to completely revolutionize our world. Many other inventions and technologies directly derived from computers and the internet accelerated the process. Smartphones were famously launched to the mainstream by the iPhone in 2007. So were fast mobile networks such as 3G, 4G and 5G. As well as tech companies such as Amazon, Google and the like, which started to become the most profitable and largest corporations in the world only in the last 10 years.

We can compare the launch of Bitcoin in 2009 with the very first computers of the 1950s and 1960s. Barely any people knew about them, and even less knew what exactly was their function. At the beginning computers were called calculators, implying that the public mostly thought about them as very powerful calculators that would simply help researchers do complicated calculations faster (something that turned out to be true, but definitely has not been the only application and use case of computers).

At the other end of the time frame, the Crypto space of today could be compared to the early tech companies of the late 1990s. Some applications of crypto are starting to clear out, exactly as it was the case for internet companies back then. Applications of the blockchain can vary greatly, exactly as pets.com had a very different vision, strategy and business model than amazon.com.

Bitcoin is the most successful application of the blockchain today and it is seen as a possible substitute of gold and store of value. At the same time, the potential of the blockchain goes well beyond that. It could make our financial industry more transparent and accessible.

If we are to consider this comparison, it took Bitcoin just about 10 years to achieve something comparable to what took computers more than 30 years. It is very well possible that the pace is going to accelerate further in the next few years, bringing more applications of this blockchain and a quick maturing of Bitcoin as a mainstream asset class.

Obviously this comparison has its limitations. It is after all pointless to try and see exact parallels between two historical periods. It might as well be that beyond Bitcoin, the blockchain still has 20 or 30 years of development before really finding its most useful applications. As all good investors know, past performance is not a valid indicator of the future.

The comparison is anyway useful, in my opinion, to understand how once again the pace of change is accelerating, at least so far. Never in history has such a disruptive technology (with close to 0 practical applications at the time of its conception) taken over and developed so quickly as in the case of Bitcoin.

Chapter 6
<u>Final thoughts about Crypto in 2021</u>

Throughout this book I have used, consciously, the words "Bitcoin", "crypto", "cryptocurrency" and "blockchain" as *de facto* synonyms. I am very well aware that this is a mistake. I think that if you have read the book until this point you did realize that these are different concepts, but I still want to spend a few paragraphs clarifying them.

As mentioned in previous chapters, the only successful application of the blockchain on a large scale, at the time of writing, is Bitcoin. Bitcoin is seen as a store of value and potential alternative to gold.

No matter what you read or are told, Bitcoin is already a store of value for the simple fact that lots of people and corporations have it exactly for this purpose. They invest in it as a hedge against fiat currencies. It is no surprise that its adoption has accelerated throughout the 2020 pandemic, since the FED and other central banks around the world have announced never before seen money printing initiatives. This is kind of a base scenario for Bitcoin, and while this remains a volatile and young asset, it has already proven to be more efficient than gold and less risk than fiat currencies.

Now, Bitcoin is one thing, crypto (as in cryptocurrencies) is another. There are hundreds of alternative coins to Bitcoin. Some have very interesting objectives and smart teams behind them. Some do not and are borderline scams. It is very well possible that some of these alternative coins will find their own applications and become huge, maybe even surpassing Bitcoin in market capitalization. One thing that I personally do not think it's very plausible at all, though, is that they will surpass Bitcoin as a means to store value. The technology behind alt-coins is negligible in that regard, because what Bitcoin really means to be a successful store of value is trust. Which is acquiring faster than any other alternative coin.

It is however possible that within other applications, alt-coins might surpass Bitcoin. We have mentioned in a previous chapter Cardano, which aims at becoming the base technology behind the financial systems for much of the developing world. This is a very different application of a cryptocurrency than what Bitcoin is today and might work very well for this project. Or it might not, despite how promising it is. It is very early to say.

Beyond Bitcoin and other cryptocurrencies, we have the blockchain. This is the technology behind all of the crypto world. I did not spend any time describing it because the reality is that its applications are still very uncertain. Again, the only successful application to date is that of Bitcoin, but it is reasonable to expect there might be many more coming in the future. Some might be other cryptocurrencies, but some might be something else altogether. Whereas we already see where Bitcoin is heading, it is simply too early to see how the blockchain will impact our lives in the years to come.

The reason why I wrote this book was to convince people that we cannot stop the development of any promising technology just because its applications seem limited today. If we adopted this approach as humanity, we would still be stuck in the african plains as hunter-gatherers.

I am a strong believer that technology is the ultimate and only savior of humanity. There is nothing else except technology that can save us from going extinct, be it because of our own idiocy (global warming or else) or by bad luck (as it happened for the dinosaurs).

At the same time I have the feeling that in recent years the public opinion has been trained to see everything in a very polarized way. Something is either good or bad, black or white. If we cannot find a reason for something to be good, then it must be bad. Or vice versa. The reality though is that most things in life are on a scale of greys. We should not lose our ability to carefully weigh pros and cons and take educated decisions.

My hope is that this book was an interesting view on the world of Crypto and, most importantly, on how we can better develop as a human species. If you found it interesting or, on the other hand, if you found it a waste of time, I invite you to write to me on Facebook at facebook.com/robertobourbonwriter. Be aware, as a bilingual author of Italian and English you might find content in a language that you do not speak! Regardless, drop me a message and let's talk. I look forward to it!